COUNTRY INSIGHTS

JAMAICA

Alison Brownlie

WAYLAND

COUNTRY INSIGHTS

BRAZIL • CHINA • CUBA • CZECH REPUBLIC • DENMARK • FRANCE
INDIA • JAMAICA • JAPAN • KENYA • MEXICO • PAKISTAN

GUIDE TO THIS BOOK

As well as telling you about the whole of Jamaica, this book looks closely at the city of Kingston and the village of Mavis Bank.

This city symbol will appear at the top of the page and information boxes each time the book looks at Kingston.

This rural symbol will appear each time the book looks at Mavis Bank.

Cover: Children in the grounds of Kingston YMCA.

Title page: Children in front of the statue of Bob Marley, the reggae superstar, in the Park of Fame, Kingston.

Contents page: Air Jamaica planes at the airport in Montego Bay, Jamaica.

Book editors: Polly Goodman and Kath Mellentin
Series editor: Polly Goodman
Designer: Tim Mayer
Consultant: Dr Tony Binns, Geography lecturer and tutor of student teachers at the University of Sussex.

First published in 1997 by
Wayland Publishers Ltd
61 Western Road, Hove
East Sussex, BN3 1JD, England

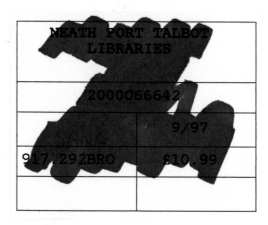
Find Wayland on the internet at http://www.wayland.co.uk

British Library Cataloguing in Publication Data
Brownlie, Alison
  Jamaica. – (Country Insights)
  1. Jamaica – Juvenile literature
  I. Title
  972.9'2'06

ISBN 0 7502 2003 1

Typeset by Tim Mayer
Printed and bound in Italy by LEGO S.p.A., Vicenza

Contents

Introducing Jamaica

What picture comes into your mind when you think of Jamaica? Do you imagine white, sandy beaches with palm trees and crystal-clear water? Jamaica does have beautiful beaches, but there is a great variety of other landscapes and people on this small island.

Jamaica is the third-largest island in the Caribbean Sea. Its population is made up of people whose ancestors came from all over the world. So the country's food, music and religions are a mixture of African, Indian, Arab and European influences.

The first people who lived in Jamaica were the Arawaks. They called the island *Xaymaca*, meaning 'land of woods and water', which is how Jamaica got its name. Christopher Columbus and the Spanish arrived in 1494, looking for gold and a route to India. Columbus thought he had reached India, which is why the Caribbean is also known as the West Indies. The Spanish forced the Arawaks to work very hard, and brought new diseases to the island, to which they had no resistance. The Arawak people died out very quickly.

Beautiful beaches and calm turquoise seas attract many tourists to Jamaica.

4

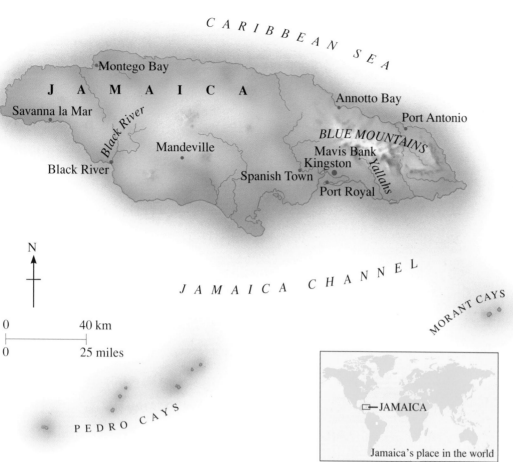

This book will take you to the city of Kingston and the village of Mavis Bank, as well as the rest of Jamaica. You can find these places on the map.

Jamaica's place in the world

▼ Young people make up a high percentage of Jamaica's population.

In 1655 the British (who were interested in growing sugar on the island) took over Jamaica. At first, there were not enough people to work on the land, so the British brought people over from Africa to work as slaves. Slavery was abolished in Jamaica in 1807, and Jamaica finally became independent in 1962. Jamaicans are proud of the way in which their ancestors fought against slavery.

JAMAICA FACTS

Population:	2.5 million
Area:	10,990 km²
Highest mountain:	Blue Mountain Peak, 2,256 m
Life expectancy:	74 years
Motto:	'Out of many, one people.'

Kingston: a modern city

Kingston is the capital of Jamaica, and is a city that teems with life. The pavements are full of street traders selling mangoes and peaches, and sky juice, a sweet fruit cordial. All kinds of music can be heard on the street corners.

Like all large cities, Kingston has office blocks, hospitals, banks and schools. Shops and department stores sell a wide range of goods, both made in Jamaica and imported from other countries. Cafés and restaurants sell specialities such as Jamaican patties, alongside Western-style fast food. Kingston also has its fair share of traffic, and the traffic jams and pollution that come with it.

Not far from the city centre are neighbourhoods which have become very rundown over the last few years. These areas, such as Trench Town and Jones Town, are dominated by street gangs and have a lot of crime. Lately, however, the government and the people who live there have done much to improve these areas.

Kingston spreads out across the coastal plain. In the distance you can see the tall buildings of the city's business district.

PORT ROYAL

The original capital of Jamaica was Port Royal. It was a very popular place with pirates, and was known as 'the wickedest place in Christendom'. In 1693, many people drowned when Port Royal was swamped by a tidal wave following an earthquake.

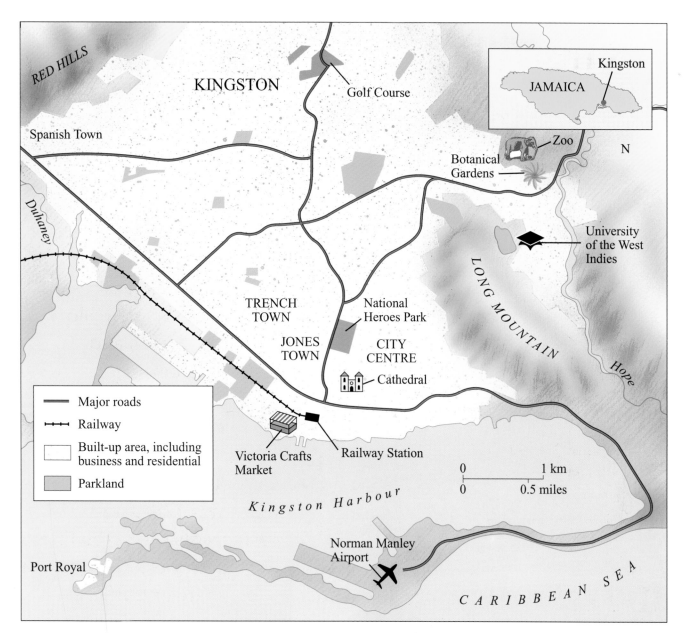

RED HILLS

KINGSTON

Golf Course

Spanish Town

JAMAICA — Kingston

Zoo

Botanical Gardens

N

Duhaney

University of the West Indies

LONG MOUNTAIN

TRENCH TOWN

National Heroes Park

JONES TOWN

CITY CENTRE

Hope

Cathedral

Railway Station

Victoria Crafts Market

— Major roads
+-+ Railway
☐ Built-up area, including business and residential
▢ Parkland

Kingston Harbour

0   1 km
0   0.5 miles

Port Royal

Norman Manley Airport

CARIBBEAN SEA

Kingston has grown very quickly over the last fifty years as Jamaica's population has increased, and many people have moved there looking for work. This has led to the development of factories which provide jobs and the goods needed in a large city like Kingston.

You can see glimpses of the Blue Mountains from all over the city of Kingston.

The village of Mavis Bank

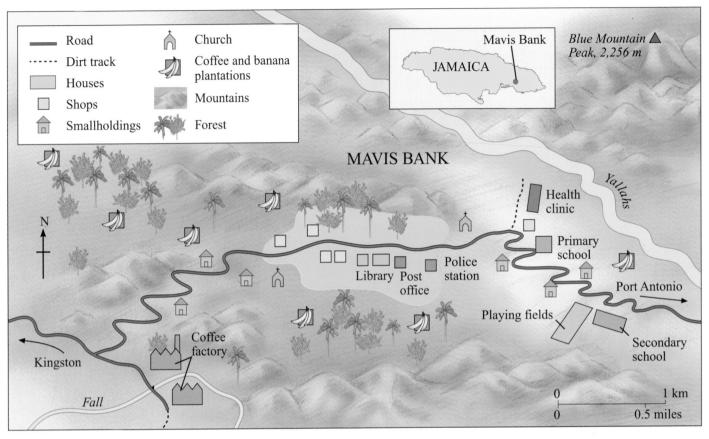

Road
Dirt track
Houses
Shops
Smallholdings
Church
Coffee and banana plantations
Mountains
Forest

Mavis Bank

JAMAICA

Blue Mountain Peak, 2,256 m

MAVIS BANK

Yallahs

Health clinic

Primary school

Port Antonio

N

Library Post office Police station

Playing fields

Secondary school

Kingston

Coffee factory

Fall

0   1 km

0   0.5 miles

Mavis Bank is a typical Jamaican village in the parish of St Andrew's, in the Blue Mountains, just north of Kingston. It hugs the side of the hills, 800 metres above sea-level. About 500 people live in Mavis Bank, but the population is very spread out. Some villagers live quite a long way from their nearest neighbours, but most people get around the village by walking.

There is not much traffic on the one road that runs through Mavis Bank.

The village has four churches, three schools, a one-person police station, a post office and a small library. There are six shops, which sell a few basic products, but they are little more than huts. A nurse runs a small clinic and the doctor visits once a week on Thursday. She travels from Gordon Town, which is about 16 kilometres away. If someone is ill on any day other than a Thursday, he or she has to travel to Kingston to see a doctor. Medical bills can be very expensive.

The road that runs through Mavis Bank is very steep, winding and full of pot-holes. Sometimes cars go over the edge of the hairpin bends. Drivers are meant to sound their horns as they go round corners to warn people. The roads are made even more dangerous by streams that run off the mountains and gush across the road. Sometimes parts of the road are washed down the hillside.

Lennox Willis Junior (below left) and his friend at the entrance to Mavis Bank.

WELCOME TO THE COMMUNITY OF MAVIS BANK

PROJECT by MRJ V S

'I was born in Mavis Bank and I really like it here. I'll probably have to go to Kingston though when I am older. There's not much work here.' – Lennox Willis Junior 10 years old (left).

9

Land and climate

Two-thirds of Jamaica is made up of hills and mountains, which are surrounded by flatter, coastal lowlands. The Blue Mountains form the eastern end of a mountain ridge that runs down the middle of the country. Rivers and streams tumble off the hills, often forming waterfalls.

Jamaica's climate is good for farming, as well as for attracting tourists. Most of the country is hot all year round, but the Blue Mountains are much cooler. December, January and February are the coolest months of the year.

The main winds come from the north-east, bringing rain. The north of the island is therefore wetter, greener and more lush than the south. In some areas of the south, cacti grow. The wettest months are usually from May to October, when tropical downpours can be expected at any time. Heavy rains are a serious problem in Jamaica. It is thought that over 80 million tonnes of soil are washed away every year in floods.

If you look closely at this picture, which was taken in the Blue Mountains, you can see hairpin bends on one of the roads.

10

Jamaican crocodiles live in the Black River, Jamaica's longest river. They lurk in the mangroves growing along the banks.

Harbour city

Kingston is bordered by the Blue Mountains to the north and the Caribbean Sea to the south. The city is slowly creeping up the foothills of the mountains as new suburbs are built. A long peninsula cradles the sheltered lagoon of Kingston harbour, where you can see ships from all over the world. Long Mountain lies to the east of the city. This is an area of high land where it is too steep to build.

'I like all the sunshine in Kingston, but it's very humid, which makes it quite uncomfortable.' – Thelma Jackson, Canadian tourist.

Kingston has one of the largest natural harbours in the world.

It is always hot in Kingston. June to September are the hottest months, but it is only a couple of degrees cooler during the rest of the year. The heat causes clouds to form on the mountains behind the city, making them look blue. This is why they are called the Blue Mountains.

KINGSTON'S CLIMATE	
Highest daily temperature:	32 °C
Lowest night-time temperature:	22 °C
Average daily hours of sunshine:	9
Average no. of rainy days a year:	69

Most of Kingston's rain falls between the months of May and November. Downpours can be sudden and very heavy. Water running off the steep slopes of the mountains, together with heavy rain, turn streets into gushing streams, deep with fast-flowing water. This causes a lot of damage, and there are many pot-holes and cracks in the roads.

A flooded road just outside Kingston. Flash floods, which turn the roads into rivers of rain-water, make driving difficult at times.

A mountain village

The steep-sided hills around Mavis Bank are easily eroded by heavy rains.

THE YALLAHS RIVER

The Yallahs river is sometimes a raging torrent. At other times it is no more than a dry river-bed filled with enormous boulders.

Mavis Bank lies in the mountains, south of the Blue Mountain Peak. The peak is visible from Mavis Bank, although it is often covered in cloud. Sometimes there is snow on it, but this is very rare.

The Yallahs river starts in the mountains, and runs close to the village on its way to the coast. The first people to settle in Mavis Bank chose to live there because the river provided a good source of clean water for drinking and washing. The river has cut a deep gorge into the land and, in places, it is difficult to get down to the river. Several small waterfalls have formed where the river flows over rocks. In order to stop the river eroding the land, walls have been built to hold back the water.

During the day, goats are often left ▶ to wander on the grass verges by the roadside. At the end of the day, they are rounded up by their owners.

When there is no rain the river dries up, leaving a series of pools where children play.

The soil around Mavis Bank is fertile and the climate is ideal for growing all kinds of crops. However, the land is very steep, and it is difficult to find flat ground for farming. Wherever it is possible, people grow fruit and vegetables. On the rockier, steeper land they keep goats and chickens.

Mavis Bank is much cooler than Kingston because it is in the mountains. The evenings can be chilly, but people still have no real need to wear a coat.

Inspecting the ▶ ripening coffee beans on a small plantation in the hills above the village. When the beans are red they are ready to be picked and sold to the factory.

Home life

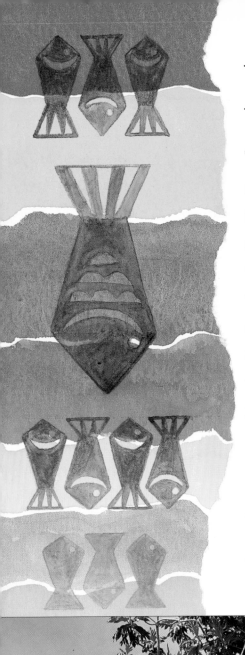

The family is very important in Jamaica. Children are often raised by a woman on her own, although aunts, grandmothers and other relations are usually close at hand to help. Children have a lot of freedom to play, but discipline is strict and children are taught to respect other people. The whole community shares the job of bringing up children, and people help with baby-sitting if the mother is at work. Anyone can tell off children if they are misbehaving.

Most people go to church regularly. Even the smallest village has a church, and most have several. In fact, Jamaica has more churches per square kilometre than any other country in the world. Some Jamaicans follow the Rastafarian religion. Followers of this religion believe that Haile Selassie I from Ethiopia is the Messiah (Jah).

The Anglican church in Black River on a Sunday morning, when most of the community go to church.

Nearly everyone speaks English, which is the language children are taught in schools. Many people also speak patois, especially in the hills and country areas. Patois is a mixture of English, African and other languages.

Jamaican food, like patois, has many influences. It is often spicy, making use of the wide range of peppers that grow on the island. Vegetables, such as plantain and bread fruit, and fruits such as mangoes and pineapples, grow abundantly. In the countryside you can just help yourself from the trees.

▼ *A plate of ackee and salt fish, Jamaica's national dish, being served for breakfast.*

TYPICAL JAMAICAN DISHES	
Jerk chicken:	Grilled chicken, prepared with a mixture of peppers, pimento, nutmeg and cinnamon.
Festival:	Deep-fried, sweet corn-bread.
Rundown fish:	Fish cooked with coconut milk and spices.

▲ *Church services are followed by Sunday school for children.*

17

Home life in Kingston

Kingston is made up of many different neighbourhoods. In the suburbs there are leafy avenues of bungalows, surrounded by gardens of tropical plants, and several homes have swimming pools. Often, there are large satellite dishes on the roofs or in the driveways. These are the areas where the wealthier Jamaicans live. Poorer people live in the shanty towns on the outskirts of the city, or in older areas in the city centre.

Mr and Mrs Smith live in Red Hills, a suburb to the north of Kingston. Their home is large, and has a balcony and a big garden where the children can play basketball.

Mrs Smith and her three children, from left to right, Kellie-Ann (fifteen), Tariq (eleven) and Anika (thirteen years old).

The Smiths have a maid who lives just a short distance away, in a small house made from weatherboard with a corrugated-iron roof.

Mrs Smith shops at the large shopping mall, but many people in Kingston buy their food from the fruit and vegetable stalls in the street markets.

Nearly all the houses in Kingston have electricity and tap water, but life is very different in the shanty towns, where the Stephenson family live. The Stephensons live in a house they built themselves, using scrap wood and plastic, and they have no electricity. Their home is built on 'captured land', meaning land that does not belong to anyone.

The Smith's house has a garden ▶ where the children can play basketball.

▲ *Even in the wealthy suburbs there is poorer housing. The Stephenson family lives in an area like the one in this picture.*

Home life in Mavis Bank

The Willis family outside their home in the centre of Mavis Bank.

'What I like about Mavis Bank is that everyone knows each other and helps each other out.' – Marion Ferris, school teacher.

Most of the houses in Mavis Bank are made of concrete, and have corrugated-iron roofs. These make a lot of noise when heavy rain falls. All the houses have electricity, and nearly everyone has a television. Only one home in Mavis Bank has a satellite dish.

Mr and Mrs Willis and their three children live in a small apartment below the bank. The building is on a small track off the main road, and is built into the side of the hill – a common practice in Mavis Bank.

◀ *There is not much flat land around Mavis Bank, so homes are often built into the steep hillside.*

▼ *Picking up the post from the post office.*

The family has a television, a radio and a telephone. It is quite dark inside the Willis' living room. The shelves are packed with ornaments, toys and books. Like the other houses in the village, their home has running water, but if they want hot water they must boil a kettle.

The shops in Mavis Bank sell items that people need on a day-to-day basis. There is butter, cheese, biscuits, tinned products, and meats such as pork, chicken and beef. One shop sells farming equipment, including machetes, spades and fertilizers. If people want to buy clothes or furniture, they must travel to Kingston. The post office at Mavis Bank sorts out the mail, but there are no deliveries. People have to go to the post office to collect their letters.

Jamaica at work

Jamaica is rich in natural resources. It has fertile land, mineral deposits and a warm climate. These resources provide many jobs in farming, the mining industry and tourism.

A large number of Jamaicans work on the land, producing sugar, bananas and coffee. These crops are sold all over the world. Families also grow many different fruits and vegetables to feed themselves, and to sell in local markets.

Edna Brown is a dumper truck driver. She is employed by a bauxite mining company, and has had this job for nine years.

TYPE OF WORK IN JAMAICA	
	Percentage of working population
Agriculture	25%
Industry	10%
Services	65%

Some Jamaicans work in the bauxite mining industry, extracting bauxite from the ground using mechanical diggers. Bauxite is a very valuable mineral, known as red gold. It is extracted from the ground as red soil, and is then processed with iron to make aluminium. Aluminium is used to make all sorts of different products, from drink cans to aircraft wings.

▲ *Many people are employed in the construction industry in Jamaica. Althea Gordon (above) is working on a new building on the University of the West Indies campus.*

Jamaica has many beautiful beaches and lots of sunshine, so it is easy to understand why many people go on holiday there. Over a million tourists visit the island each year. Tourism creates a huge number of jobs in hotels and restaurants for waiters, cleaners, security guards and cooks. Some Jamaicans find work as tourist guides, showing visitors round the island. Other people make souvenirs to sell to the tourists.

Many Jamaicans do not have a regular job. Instead, they do odd jobs here and there. Many people move to the towns to look for work, and some even go abroad.

Moving barrels of coffee in a ▶ coffee factory. The growing and processing of coffee, bananas and sugar for sale abroad provides many jobs.

Working in Kingston

> 'The hotel where I work is always busy with tourists from all over the world. I like meeting so many different people all the time.' – Winston Johnson, security guard.

Many people in Kingston, and from the surrounding region, travel to the city centre each day to work in the banks, insurance companies, offices, shops and factories. They work as managers, secretaries and computer operators. In factories, people operate machinery producing goods to be sold in Jamaica and abroad.

People travel to work on hot, crowded buses and in private cars, creating traffic jams on the main roads during the rush hour.

Mr and Mrs Smith both have jobs and are well off. Mr Smith runs his own construction company, building houses, while Mrs Smith is an estate agent. They both drive into the centre of Kingston every day from their home in the suburbs.

Winston Johnson is a security guard at the Sandhurst Hotel in Kingston. He is employed by a private security firm.

People who come to Kingston looking for work are often disappointed. Many find it difficult to find regular employment, so they do whatever work they can. Sheldon Brown is fifteen years old. He earns money by washing car windscreens while the cars stop at traffic lights. Many women, known as higglers, sell souvenirs and goods such as make-up and hair ornaments on the city's streets. Some higglers even travel to the USA to buy the goods they sell.

On the waterfront people make things to sell to the tourists. Here visitors can buy brightly painted wood carvings of Jamaican parrots and fish, printed fabrics and other colourful souvenirs of their stay on the island.

▲ *Dotty Donaldson on her first day at work at Velma's Gift Shop, on Kingston's waterfront.*

▼ *Sheldon Brown, fifteen years old, busy at work in the wealthy suburb of New Kingston.*

Working in Mavis Bank

'On Fridays, I take the bus to Kingston with my baskets of mangoes. I sell them on the streets.' – Maria Jarrett, farmer.

Jobs where people work from nine to five are unusual in Mavis Bank. Some people make furniture, mend cars, or hire out their car, but most of these are not permanent jobs.

Nearly every household has a small plot of land, on which they grow some of the food they need. Between the rows of fruit, cabbages and lettuces people also grow six or seven coffee bushes. The beans harvested from these bushes, and from larger coffee plantations, are sold to the Mavis Bank coffee factory. Here the coffee beans are sorted, washed, ground and packed by the villagers, ready to be sold all over the world.

The amount of work at the coffee factory varies according to the season, so jobs may only be available for a short time.

Packing coffee into foil bags inside the Mavis Bank coffee factory. The factory employs between 150–250 people from the village, depending on the season.

Blue Mountain coffee is one of the best in the world, and is sold to Japan, the USA and Europe. Mavis Bank is lucky to have the coffee factory but there are still not enough jobs, and some young people hang around playing dice to pass the time of day.

Most of the villagers keep a few animals, such as goats and chickens. They let the goats wander during the day or tether them by the side of the road on a narrow stretch of grass.

▲ Coffee beans being washed at the coffee factory. You can see the Blue Mountain Peak in the distance.

◄ One of the shop-keepers in the village. Mavis Bank is a small village, so he knows most of his customers by name.

Going to school

Almost all children up to the age of eleven years old go to school in Jamaica, and nearly every adult can read and write. The Jamaican school system is considered to be very good. Some people, who have moved abroad to live, send their children back to Jamaica to go to school. However, the government now has less money to spend on schools. This means that teachers' salaries are low and some schools are very overcrowded. In these schools, children have to take it in turns to go to school – some go in the morning and others go in the afternoon.

School usually starts at 8.00 am and finishes by 1.30 pm, because it is too hot to study in the afternoon. All children wear school uniform, which their parents must buy, and the teachers are very strict. Jamaicans believe in discipline. Strangers will stop children in the street and ask them why they are not at school. Everyone knows that one of the best ways for children to do well and get on in life is to have a good education.

Children sing the Jamaican national anthem every morning before lessons begin.

Schoolchildren at ▶ the start of their morning break after the first lessons of the day.

Places in secondary schools (from twelve years old) are limited, and children have to pass an exam to get accepted. Some poorer children cannot go, even if they pass the exam, because they have to help their families by working instead.

▼ *Young children learn to read and write from an early age. Yannique Brown is five years old and is learning how to write her name.*

Most schools are run by the government, but there are a few private ones where parents must pay, and some that are run by the churches. Rastafarian schools teach children about Africa, and Marcus Garvey, a Jamaican who fought against racism, as well as their usual subjects.

School in Kingston

'I'm in my school's swimming team. We have a really big playing field, where many other games are played.'
– John Bennett, 11 years old.

Children share a joke on their way to school in Kingston.

There is a greater choice of schools in Kingston than in Mavis Bank. For example, parents can choose to send their children to a single-sex school, which they cannot do in the country-side.

Most Kingston schools are better equipped than those in the villages, and the school buildings are more modern. Nearly all of them have computers. A typical high school has about 1,500 pupils. There are usually between thirty-six and forty-five pupils in each class. In more crowded schools, one class may sit facing one way, while a different class faces the other way. In poorer areas, special schools have been set up for younger children, to help them get a better start.

Schools award certificates to pupils for sporting achievement, for doing well in school subjects, and also for good citizenship, for example helping people who are less well off than themselves.

Mrs Smith takes her children to school by car in the morning. The journey takes about half an hour. Many children in Kingston go to school by car, but others walk or take the bus. After school, the Smith children go to a friend's house while their mother is still working. They usually have plenty of homework to do. All the Smith children hope to go to the University of the West Indies in Kingston when they finish school. This is the largest university in the Caribbean.

Passing exams is very important, ▶ *and pupils are expected to work hard.*

School in Mavis Bank

In Mavis Bank there is a nursery school for children from three to six years, a primary school for six to twelve-year-olds, and a secondary school for children from twelve to fifteen years old. The three Willis children walk to school every day. They all go to the primary school, although Todea-Kay will go to the secondary school next year.

Their school is a long, single-storey building. There are slats in the windows instead of glass, which keep out the hot rays of the sun while letting in cool breezes. Even in primary school, children are expected to work hard, and they have about two hours of homework every night.

▼ *Children outside the secondary school in Mavis Bank. The school motto, 'Forward for the best', is written in the centre of the sign.*

Many pupils stay behind after school to play football on the schools sports ground. This is the only flat piece of land in the village.

The secondary school takes pupils from a wide area. Some children arrive by bus, but others, who live far from the bus route, or who cannot afford the fare, must walk. They may have to walk several kilometres and it can take some children up to two hours each way. It is difficult for these children to continue to go to school when they live so far away, and also need to help out at home.

▲ A bus carries children from villages nearby to the schools in Mavis Bank.

'I want to be a nurse when I'm older. I'll have to go to Kingston to get qualified.'
– Jennifer Brown, 10 years old.

Jamaica at play

Leisure time is very important to Jamaicans. Music, sport and any event where people can get together are all very popular. Having a barbecue of jerk chicken on the beach, going to a party or just getting together for a chat are an essential part of Jamaican daily life.

Reggae music was born on the island of Jamaica. Bob Marley helped to make this style of music popular all over the world, but it is especially loved by the Jamaicans. In the summer, a big reggae festival called 'Sunsplash' is held in Montego Bay. Fans travel from all over the world to hear their favourite reggae stars perform. Bob Marley died in 1981, and there is now a statue of him in the Park of Fame in Kingston.

Jamaica's main cultural festival takes place during the weeks leading up to Independence Day on 6 August. Plays are performed all over the island, along with music and dance shows. Everyone is expected to join in!

The statue of Bob Marley outside his house (near right), and a billboard welcomes visitors to 'Bob Marley's Jamaica' (far right).

Jamaicans are extremely proud of their cultural heritage, but many US-style leisure activities are becoming increasingly popular. This is because Jamaicans watch a lot of American programmes on satellite television. Some older Jamaicans are not happy about this, and refuse to buy satellite dishes. Even so, US sports such as basketball are played more and more, although cricket is still the country's number one game. Athletic activities are also very popular. For such a small country, Jamaica has been very successful in international track and field events. Merlene Ottey, for example, who is one of the world's best sprinters, has taken part in many competitions and has won medals at two Olympic Games.

▲ Basketball is growing more and more popular in Jamaica.

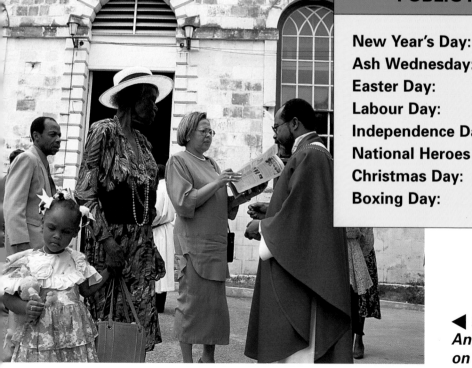

PUBLIC HOLIDAYS IN JAMAICA	
New Year's Day:	1 January
Ash Wednesday:	March/April
Easter Day:	March/April
Labour Day:	23 May
Independence Day:	First Monday in August
National Heroes Day:	Third Monday in October
Christmas Day:	25 December
Boxing Day:	26 December

◀ People chatting outside the Anglican church in Black River on a Sunday morning.

Leisure time in Kingston

For those who can afford it, every kind of leisure activity is available in Kingston. The capital city has sports stadiums, swimming pools, two drive-in cinemas and many theatres. In the shopping malls in the suburbs, there are lots of video arcades, where young people like playing on the machines.

At the weekend, people like to forget the noise and crowds of the city by going to the beach, or hiking in the mountains. Some people drive up to Mavis Bank and start their trek from there. Others travel all the way to Black River to see the crocodiles.

'At the weekends, we sometimes go to Hellshire beach for a barbeque. Our whole family goes. That's about fifteen people.' – Maria da Costa, supermarket manager.

Playing tennis at the Liguanea Club in New Kingston. This is a private sports club.

◀ Visitors to Kingston's National Art Gallery look at an exhibition about life in a Kingston shanty town.

Comedies and pantomimes are performed in theatres, such as the Ward Theatre. These shows are often based on the stories of Anancy, a cunning spider who is the hero of Caribbean fables. Kingston also has a national art gallery and a museum of culture where people can enjoy Jamaica's rich heritage. In the cool of the evenings, people often sit out on their verandas and chat about the events of the day.

▼ Children in the grounds of the Kingston YMCA. There are lots of activities to choose from all through the summer holidays.

In the centre of Kingston and in the poorer areas there are fewer parks and open spaces where children can play. Instead, they play on the streets, or on any empty piece of land they can find.

Leisure time in Mavis Bank

Music and singing form an important part of church services.

If you went to Mavis Bank on a Sunday morning, you would see people on their way to church in their very best clothes. Church services include loud, lively singing – everyone joins in! After church, some families go down to the river to swim. Deep bathing pools have been made where villagers have dammed the river.

Unlike Kingston, there are no cinemas or pleasure parks in Mavis Bank. People make their own entertainment, and children are very clever at making the best of what they have. They roll up rags and tie them into bundles to make footballs, and use small coconuts for cricket balls. The Willis children enjoy making their own games. Lennox Junior makes kites out of bamboo and scrap paper, while Todea-Kay and Natoya play in the streams and woods around their home.

'Sundays after church are a good chance to catch up with everyone.' – Cherol Green, 18 years old (left).

Adults gather outside the shops to pass the time of day and catch up on the latest news. Sometimes they chew a small piece of sugar-cane while they chat. The pace of life is slow and not much happens.

In the evening most people in Mavis Bank watch television or a video. Miss Patterson, the local librarian, is concerned that people don't read as many books as they used to, especially the young.

TRADITIONAL TALES

Stories about Anancy, the spiderman, were brought from the west coast of Africa by slaves over 200 years ago. These stories are often told to children at bedtime.

▲ *Lennox Willis Junior and his friend play with a toy they have made from an old wheel.*

◄ *The Jamaican national flag on the wall of the Mavis Bank library.*

The future

Although Jamaica is rich in most resources, it has to import energy, including petrol for cars and oil for industry. This is very expensive for the country. In the future Jamaica may be able to meet some of its energy needs by using solar and wind power. Some houses already have solar panels and wind pumps, and the government wants to expand their use in the future.

With the increasing use of satellite television, it is likely that the USA will have a greater influence on the Jamaican way of life in the future – the food people eat, the clothes they wear and the music they listen to. Young people are particularly affected. Some Jamaicans are worried about this trend. Mrs Smith will not buy a satellite dish because she feels her children should learn more about Jamaican than American culture.

A satellite dish points towards the USA, bringing American television programmes to Jamaica.

▲ A sports shop in New Kingston. Jamaica's sportsmen and women look set to continue ranking among the best in the world.

Jamaica has a very young population. Large numbers of these young people no longer wish to work in the countryside, but find it difficult to get a job in town. Some go to live in other countries such as Canada and the USA, where they can earn more money. Unfortunately, it is those who are well-educated, such as teachers, nurses and doctors, who leave Jamaica to find a new life abroad. It is important that these people stay in their country in order to help it develop and prosper in the future.

◀ A tour boat on the Black River. Tourism is vital to Jamaica's future.

41

The future of Kingston

Kingston has changed a great deal in the last twenty years. It has grown very quickly, with new office blocks, factories and suburbs spreading out and up into the foothills. Kingston's rapid growth has made some people better off, but it has also created a large number of poor people, and the gap between the two groups is constantly growing.

Pollution is a problem that faces nearly all large modern cities, and Kingston is no exception. Heavy traffic affects the health of Kingstonians and their ability to get about their city. On most days a smog lies over the city. As more people become wealthier, and buy cars, this problem will worsen unless special action is taken.

There is always building work going on somewhere in Kingston, as the city continues to grow.

CITY GROWTH

In just a few years, the Hellshire area has grown from an uninhabited headland to an extension of Kingston. Some people are unhappy about buildings taking over the natural areas.

◀ *Many people who move to Kingston build temporary homes like these, which are in the mainly wealthy suburb of Red Hills.*

As more people come to Kingston in search of jobs, new houses must be built for them. Otherwise the city's shanty towns will keep on growing, along with poverty and crime. However, many projects have already been started to make life better for people living in the poorer areas of Kingston. Many young people from the shanty towns and downtown areas are now being trained in the skills necessary to do some of the new jobs in the city. There are courses that develop computer skills, and others that teach people how to run their own businesses. These courses are often taken by people want to improve their lives.

▼ *Buses in Kingston are usually crowded. Instead of running to a timetable, they set off when they are full.*

The future of Mavis Bank

Unlike Kingston, Mavis Bank has not changed a great deal in the last few years, and some people think it won't change very much in the future. It faces the challenge that all small villages in Jamaica must face – a decreasing population as many young people leave the village to find work in the towns and cities. There are a few jobs for young people in the coffee factory, but not enough for everyone. As a result, unemployment is high. Young people are attracted to Kingston not only by the possibility of a job, but also by the 'bright lights' and excitement it offers. By comparison, Mavis Bank is very quiet!

Sorting through the coffee beans to make sure only the best are used. The coffee factory will continue to provide much needed work for people in Mavis Bank.

Mavis Bank is not far from Kingston, but the road between the two is in bad condition and the journey can take up to two hours. If the road were improved, more people would be encouraged to live in Mavis Bank because they would be able to travel to Kingston for work.

Some new houses are being built in the village – a sign that people want to live in Mavis Bank – and although many people complain about the cost of living, most are generally better off than they used to be. Nearly every family has a television, and it is likely that more will get satellite dishes in the near future.

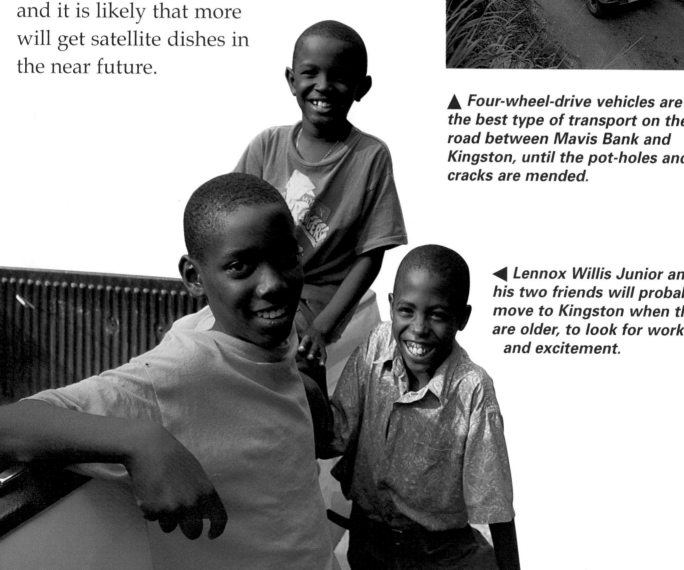

▲ Four-wheel-drive vehicles are the best type of transport on the road between Mavis Bank and Kingston, until the pot-holes and cracks are mended.

◄ Lennox Willis Junior and his two friends will probably move to Kingston when they are older, to look for work and excitement.

45

Glossary

Ancestors The people we are related to who have lived before us, including our grandparents, great-grandparents and any relations before them.

Community spirit The way people who live in the same place help each other and work together.

Crops Plants that are grown to produce food.

Fertile Fertile land is rich in the nutrients plants need to grow well.

Jerk chicken A traditional Jamaican chicken dish, cooked with lots of spices.

Lagoon An area of water separated from the sea by a sand-bank or a piece of land.

Machetes Small axes used to chop wood.

Mangroves Trees and shrubs that grow in mud on river banks and on the sea-shore in the tropics. They have long roots which grow above the ground.

Minerals Substances such as gold, coal or bauxite which occur naturally in the ground, and can be obtained by mining.

Peninsula A piece of land surrounded on three sides by water.

Plantain A fruit that is similar to the banana, but tastes less sweet.

Plantation An area of land that is planted with a single crop or type of tree.

Pollution Damage caused to the environment by substances such as poisonous chemicals or toxins from traffic and factories.

Pot-holes Deep holes in road surfaces.

Racism The belief that one race of people are better than another, and the treatment of others influenced by this belief.

Reggae music Popular West Indian music with a strong beat.

Resources The things a country possesses that are useful to it. Sunshine, bauxite and people are some of Jamaica's resources.

Self-sufficient Able to supply the things that one needs to live, without help from other people.

Shanty towns Poor areas on the outskirts of cities where people have built their own homes from scrap materials.

Slavery When people who are forced to work for little or no pay. Jamaican slaves belonged to their owners, and could be bought and sold. There are still slaves today in some parts of the world.

Solar power A method of obtaining electricity from the heat and light of the sun. It is very expensive to set up, but cheap to run.

Souvenirs Something bought on holiday to remind you of your visit.

Suburbs Areas on the edges of large towns and cities consisting mainly of houses and shops.

Further information

Books to Read

Anancy Spiderman: Twenty Caribbean Folk Stories by James Berry (Walker, 1989)

Caribbean Stories by Robert Hull (Wayland, 1994)

Focus on the Caribbean by Cas Walker (Evans, 1992)

Fodor's Exploring the Caribbean by James Hamlyn (Fodor's Travel Publications, 1994)

Habitats: Islands by Julia Waterlow (Wayland, 1995)

On the Map: The Caribbean by David Flint (Macdonald Young Books, 1992)

Our Country: Jamaica by Simon Scoones (Wayland, 1992)

People and Places: The Caribbean and its People by T. W. Mayer (Wayland, 1994)

World Focus: Jamaica by John Barraclough (Oxfam, 1995)

Useful Address

Jamaica Tourist Board, 1-2 Prince Consort Road, London, SW7 2BZ

Sources

All the statistics for this book were taken from the following sources:
UNESCO Statistical Yearbook, 1993;
UN World Statistics in Brief, 14th edition; World Bank World Tables, 1994;
UNICEF, The State of the World's Children, 1995;
UN Human Development Report, 1994.

Acknowledgements

The author would like to thank Nicky Richardson of the Jamaica Tourist Board and Philip Chavannes for information and guidance.

Picture Acknowledgements

All photographs, except those listed below, are by Howard J. Davies.
Page 28, 33 (bottom): Alison Brownlie;
Pages 29, 31 (bottom): Wayland Picture Library (David Cumming).
All maps are by Hardlines.
Border artwork by Kate Davenport.

Index

Page numbers in **bold** refer to photographs.